♡ Larry, brother!
love you!
To memories!
♡ hugs,
Marc
6-2015

Blue.River.Apple.

"Wow! I am blown away and brought to tears. My own mother can no longer communicate except for a few words or an occasional sentence. Most of the time I can tell by her eyes she is in another place. She stills smiles a lot which helps as I can believe that she is happy. There are times I know she wants to tell me things and I can guess by a word she says and the circumstance around us what she wants to say. Thank you for this book, as this has helped me."

Elizabeth Lonseth,
author of "A Gradual Disappearance, "
elizabethlonsethnovels.com

Blue. River. Apple.

Copyright © 2014, Nancy Nelson
Cover Image: Cynthia Carbajal
Internal Design: Julie Dickinson

978-0-9904266-0-8
$14.95 US

Blue. River. Apple.

an exploration of Alzheimer's through poetry

-Nancy Nelson

Table of Contents

In memory of Robert Williams, my dad and confidant, who died in 2002 from complications of Alzheimer's disease. May I always feel his shoulder of love by my side.

I would like to express my love and appreciation:

To my parents, both deceased and looking down from above, Madge Mason and Robert Williams.

To my daughters, Michelle and Jennifer, who make life worth living.

To my grandchildren, Brayden, Delaney, Rachel Anne and Jack who bring laughter and love daily.

To all of my immediate family cheering me on.

To my extended family who never let a piece of paper dictate their love for me.

To my dear friends, some go back 65 years, who just make my life better.

To Patricia, for her tireless toil, general brilliance, and high tolerance to her cousin's learning curve.

To our Writing Critique Group. If it were not for them, I'd never be where I am today. A tremendous thank you to Deborah, Stephen, Sue, Gail and Donelle.

**I'd like to gratefully acknowledge key
Blue. River. Apple. contributors:**

"In loving memory of my Mom, Diane Snyder . . .
my friend, my mentor, my inspiration!"
Cynthia and Tim Ganey, Las Vegas, NV

"In loving memory of my favorite cousin, Betty
Wheeler, who passed away from Alzheimer's—
and recently her sister, Phyllis Sodaro, who has
been diagnosed with senile dementia."
Ed Healy, Las Vegas, NV

"In loving recognition of my mother, Betty Beason,
who leads by example each day and always in a
pay-it-forward lifestyle. I love you, Mom."
Dave Beason, Las Vegas, NV

"In loving thoughts for my aunt, Lulu Prestbo."
Kathie Paustian, Las Vegas, NV

Jim and Shanley Lett, Lopez Island, WA

Kristine Agers, Las Vegas, NV

Be

Be
Be Still
Be Still and Know
God is here
In me and in you.
Handing off love to comfort us
He wants us to grow

~ Unknown ~

Accomplishments

"People of accomplishment rarely sit
back and let things happen to them.
They go out and happen to things."

~ Leonardo da Vinci ~

Silence

"Learn to get in touch with the
silence within yourself and know
everything in this life has a purpose."

~ Elizabeth Kubler-Ross ~

Foreword

I was honored when Nancy Nelson asked me to write this foreword to her book of poetry, Blue. River. Apple. Nancy has early-onset Alzheimer's disease. Merely by deciding to chronicle her thoughts and daily experiences in verse, Nancy has enhanced her own life. By choosing to share her poems with the public, she will enhance the lives of countless others.

Like Nancy, I am the daughter of a parent diagnosed with Alzheimer's disease. I know how easy it is to mourn lost normalcy and worry about which skill or memory might disappear tomorrow. Gradually, however, I have learned the value of staying in the present and appreciating today's possibilities.

My mother lives in a nursing home and recently turned 90 years of age. One evening, when ordinary conversation with my mother no longer worked, I prayed to God for a way to connect with her. He guided me to the Lord's Prayer. I was so delighted when she remembered the words! For years, every Sunday when my brother would call me from her room, we would say the Prayer together. Now I say it to her and hope she can respond, "Amen."

It is hard to see this wonderful woman, once so active and involved with community and family, sit quietly and—to outward appearances—idle. My mother is frail, needs a wheelchair, and cannot care for herself any more. Yet I believe she is happy in her world. She attends church at the nursing home each Sunday with family members who are able to come. Sometimes she remembers one of the songs; her favorite is "The Old Rugged Cross." I am blessed that, through her love of God, these treasured links of communication remain for us to share.

Nancy's poems bring her daily experiences to life with honesty, power, and clarity. She is an optimist with courage who confronts her fears and marches forth.

Through her writing, I get glimpses of what my mother might have thought or felt. These glimpses of the unknown bring me comfort and alleviate my fear. In addition, the poems in Blue. River. Apple. stand alone as works of art, inspired and pure.

Barbara Cegavske
Nevada State Senator
August 2, 2014

PREFACE

One day my world changed abruptly.

In September 2013, my daughter and I sat in a doctor's
office tightly holding hands, sweaty and nervous,
waiting for the outcome of medical tests and final
opinions. We were expecting better, but received a
diagnosis of the most dreaded kind.

Early-onset Alzheimer's.

Dementia translates as "deprived of mind." Confirmation
that I was to follow in my father's footsteps jarred me in
ways I never imagined.

Since hearing the news, I awaken between 3 and 5 in the
morning. Zero dark thirty is when my eyes fly open and
I'm full-on aware. The words that normally tumble off my
tongue now flow feverishly by pencil over a yellow-lined
pad—as though I am possessed. And I write. Poetry.

In my poems, I recapture times over the last seven
months where I am sure my life is over; and on better
days, I know it is not. I explore my frustrations and
share my views. I expose the gut-wrenching feeling
that hits me when I've missed an appointment or the
many occasions I cannot remember a name or face of
someone I spent time with just yesterday. Intermittently,
I'm confused and cannot figure out a word for the life of
me; then sadly I stammer and falter with the elocution—
often feeling it might have been better to keep quiet.
This book is a snapshot of who I was on the day I wrote

each poem. The emotional heart of these poems lies in an attempt to find my own traumatized self-regard as each day seems to bring on a new challenge.

Spying on my future and relating day-to-day realities through poetry has been cathartic, though sobering. I'm diligent to splash on a smile, square my shoulders, speak out, listen, and accept a stage description, like "high functioning." I dig deep for gratitude. Inside, I cringe and I cry. Millions of Americans struggle in silence, afraid to divulge their secret ... I'm standing up to be counted ... for them and for me.

So if I can help you, your spouse or life partner, your parents, siblings, friends, extended family members, caregiver—God Bless Our Caregiver—then this is a win-win. We'll walk through the fear of diagnosis and the hard cold dementia realities together.

Humbly,
Nancy Nelson

Blue. River. *Apple*.

Today's journey:

> Develop courage,
> Splash on a smile,
> Be who I want to be,
> Not afraid of who I am becoming.

To awake at night, fearful of forgetting
Important and precious things like ...
People. Dates. Times. Appointments.
I am not in control. Please help me, God.

Thoughts jumble, words **d i s a p p e a r.**
Times mix up, promises go astray.
When I hear, *"Where are you?" "Are you coming?"*
Eyes water, stomach churns, humbled in disbelief.
I know I have done it again!

Do I stay home, cancel, quit?
Or fight for right of passage through the fog?
Silently, I say, I am not what I appear.
I am sorry for what you see.

> Breathe in courage,
> Splash on a smile,
> Struggle to remember ...
> I must find pieces of myself and revel in who I know I am.
> Chin up, treading lightly in new uncharted waters.

At times, I catch sideways glances, back and forth.
Perhaps, even, your voice impatient. I *understand.*
But, wait, we stand together, separate.
Can you hear me? I have so much to tell you.

I try to mask the imperfections.
A dab of foundation, a blush of pink.
Dressed in clothes, jewelry, and resolve
Daily, though, I have to make sense of where I am.

On the sliding scale of ... **Blue.** River. *Apple*.

I want to be Positive.
I **am** Productive.
I **am** Loving and Beloved.
I **am** Grateful, Creative, Alive.
Therefore ...
I **am** blessed with a voice to tell my inner story.

Blue. River. *Apple*.

time is shorter
THAN USUAL

A sad knowing.
There is a lack of distance.

Family fractured
In discord.
Devastating, silly.
It is.

———————————

time is shorter
THAN USUAL

———————————

Not an elastic band,
Able to **stretch** on and on.
But a string with an end.

What to do in this knowledge?
Shut up? Sit down?
Stand aside as a vessel without a sea?
"No!" calls my door from within.
"Don't close!"

I am here.
I have so much to do.

Family peace, harmony,

love.

Apparently
I didn't do it well.
The most important of all things,

A family bond that binds.
In times of storm and calm
Gather together, not apart.

I didn't do it well.

Courageously stand out.
Be mighty I must.
"Oh no, I'm not done."
In complete deep love.
One blink means yes,
Two blinks mean no.
Help me to remember.

———————————

time is shorter
THAN USUAL

———————————

I AM WARRIOR

Silence. Darkness reigns.
Garage door grinds shut.

Did I forget to close it?

– Sssh, sleep, it is okay.

I lay awake.
Fear resurfaces.
Inner tunnels of my mind ...

Did I leave our house unprotected?

– Sssh, sleep.

Night passes.
Do I ask or lay silent?
WARRIOR *or Coward?*
Eyes close, I snuggle in.
No decision is a decision.
Wrong choice, **WARRIOR**.

Prepared to do better,
But caught in between ...
Did I? Or didn't I?
Please help me ... remember.

Go ahead,
Take a chance, ask.

"Son, did I forget to close the garage door?"
"No, Mom, I came in late."

Remember, **WARRIOR**,
Always ask.
Stand tall, straight, and accountable
Again.

My shoulders square,
My jaw relaxes.
My heart sings!
I am who I want to be

I AM WARRIOR.

It's Seven O'Clock

On the dot, *Seven O'Clock*

I felt my name being called.
From far and away.
I was not present, I could not go.

It's better, really,
I know.

A family team
Working together
Like a well-oiled sewing machine,
Uniting pieces and parts,

My family quilt, PLUS ONE.

It's all about me,
A gathering.
Close encounters, STITCHING EACH AS ONE.
An author, dear friend, and my kids in tow.
Eye-to-eye contact, united in cause,

JOINED in a way as never before.

Details unwanted,
But, coming they were
To the ears of my baby chicks,
Hearing what they didn't want to know,
Uncomfortable words, tears,
About disease ... and me.

Surely you're mistaken.
They pondered.

Not my mom, my grandmom,
Perfectly TAILORED, *straightlaced as she?*
Her?
She'd **never, ever,** UNRAVEL that way.

But wait … you're saying … she'll lose control?

It's Seven O'Clock

I poured me a stiff one
Like the lonely alcoholic who cannot quit at one.
Away from home, I drank that double shot—

And more than one!

Thirty Days In

Diagnosis. Cold hard facts set in.

[
Shipwrecked.
Body strong.
Brain, hole-y, unhealthy.
]

I glimpse ahead.
Summer's going,
Winter's approaching.

The undeniable truth feels like
Mind's fading. The slap stings my face.
As hesitation sets in
And confidence wanes,
My landscape now stark and wintery,

How to prepare?

Push back the curtain of fear.
Open the shutters.
Search for the light.

A spark—hope, fascination, heart.

Then, right in front of me, out the window,
Fifty, maybe more,
Baby coots, the robust and the runts alike
Upend themselves, all diving
With joyful abandon.
I wonder, what makes them so resilient?
Birds hidden in trees, twittering.
The view from this side of the shutters is not all bad.

God's power, all is well.
From tiny creatures water-bound
To cheering for the underdog.
From where I stand, I believe,
That looks to be me.

A glimpse behind, a glimpse ahead.
Now is the time to be grateful,
And count my blessings.

One. Two. Three.

SEARCHING for Signs

Goddammit.
(Pleeeeeease, no disrespect meant.)
But *where, where is my phone*?
Madly thrusting through my purse, car seat, floor.

In this morning of people I met, errands I ran,
Somewhere, I have left it behind!

AGAIN.

I'm as helpless as the mournful train whistle
Before it escapes down the lonely, distant track.

AGAIN.

Whooo! Whooo! Whooo!

How do I *function*?

I cannot even remember to hang on to
A phone.
My memoryline.
Am I *losing it*?
Am I *the fragile train whistle that I hear*?

Times ago
I could have shrugged my shoulders,
Shook my head,
Laughed.

Today. Not so much.
I'm hurting from way within,

Screaming full bore.
Stop it!
Don'tcha get it?
I'm not laughing anymore.

If only the memoryline would fray less,
Just deliver a personal reprimand or two.
God Damn It.
(I mean no disrespect.)
But ... I really, really,
Don't want to lose, misplace, leave behind,
Forget **MY PHONE!**

   EVER AGAIN.

In other Words...

You may ask, *what is presenile dementia?*
Too simply and from a novice ...I read

⎡ 1) Any of various forms of dementia... ⎤
⎣ 2) AD, Alzheimer's Disease.   ⎦

They say, brain and mental deterioration
Causing patients the inability
To communicate, interact.
Affects mid-lifer's routine drastically.
Often, frustration displays in ways
Themselves and their families have not seen—
Outbursts called behavioral disturbances—
That eventually requires caregivers 24/7.

In other words . . .

It is very disquieting, **indeed**, **indeed**. Indeed.

And if that isn't enough,
I've been diagnosed with symptoms—
But let's make light of it—I'll simply call it the A's.
It has less profound meaning to me, that way.
I'm sure it's just an interim coping mechanism,
To the diagnosis—early on-set A's—in beginning stages.
Could it be possible that this pure and unadulterated
Life-altering malaise is living rent-free in my very own head?

And if that isn't enough,
A snarl of nerve fibers are built around a central
Deposit of aluminosilicates—ah-ha, aluminum!
Discontinue the use of those aluminum pots and pans.
And eat a plant-based diet, walk briskly daily,
Keep the mind busy, etc., etc., etc.

Take vitamins, no, take drugs, read a lot, be social,
Douse in coconut oil, run, take yoga, relax, be social,
Hug a dog, get 7 to 8 hours sleep every night, etc., etc., etc.

Don't be depressed–**heavens no!**

In other words . . .

Whew! I feel like late afternoon with sunlight disappearing
Behind a bank of darkened clouds and nighttime's
Stormy skies are coming ......
Thank God I have my loving family, and friends.

Thank God.

Beachfront Tides

In my childhood

Thousands of weekends and summers spent on
Camino Island in the beautiful Pacific Northwest.
From nippy cool early morn 'til dark,
Climbing the shoreline's hilly sand dunes,

Or, skipping along in solitary, listening to ...

The magical salty tidewaters calling from
Their ebb and flow.
By inbound waves of the sea
Forcibly overtaking shoreline's crevices, including
Splashes over my toes firmly planted
In the wet sand's softness.
Joyfully gazing into the blue-green,
Mesmerized as my pants
Darkened with water,
The deeper I'm in,
My mindful watching intentionally absorbs
Only what the water is willing to give me.

However, unlike then, today I'm more aware that

What comes in must go outward ... again to sea.
It makes me think—
It is the same with my conscious aging mind.
It recedes away from shore, from me, and
I'm left standing wet-and-sandy-footed—unprotected.
The water's gone—the tide is simply out.
My unmanageable brain is away, at times leaving me
Cold and left behind.

Those years as a kid running up and down the shore

Give me warm and nurturing flashbacks
And I realize I am as lucky as ever a girl can be
To have walked the beachfront free.
Today I appreciate that what goes out
Might not come back in,
And certainly not always in the same
Condition as when it left.
I find that true for me.

SIDE EFFECTS

The good ol' Doc—
Important is he
As he stands with his back
Addressing the x-rays,
Not my daughter, Jenn, and me.

We're hearing … good news.
We're high-fiving, we are,
I'm squeezing Jenn's hand;
And, she mine.

Doc turned—eyes offhand,

　"You have early-onset A's!"
　"You'll begin Aricept, today."

Message delivered!
"We're good, it's fine."

But Doc, wait!
That's it—stick a fork in me and
I'm done?

Like a petulant child needing
Some parental control,
My face contorted in disbelief.
My lip bit to blood in my rush to say,
"Have you seen the side effects?"

From my heart to Doc's unyielding ears,
My mouth dry, making spit hard to find.
Though belabored, my words not withheld,
"NO drugs today, they're not for me!"

His reply, *"It slows down the process."*

Pleeese, just how do they know that?
I've listened, read articles, and attended Care Groups.
There is a resounding—You really can't tell ...
About these drugs.
Pill-bottle instructions read,
"Encouraged to Report Side Effects."

Really?Are you able to ask me?
If yes ... Do you believe me?
If I cannot speak, no comprendre,
You go ahead, present it to me ...
Like it's some prize I'm so lucky to win.
Oh, I understand, yes I do!
I don't have those malfunctioning parts
Mentioned on that Pharma List.
... But assuredly, I will.

At ten minutes past full-minded,
It makes me downright
Punching Bag Mad,
Antagonistic,
Angry,
Mind-Bogglingly Distraught to think...

"It's for my own good!"

The **dіɹ⊥**

A bone-crunching plummet to the floor
Smacks me hard on callous, unforgiving,
Commercial carpeting,
Like a boxer knocked to the mat, I come to, dazed.
How did I get to this place of looking up
With eyes that won't focus?

The boxer knows. The difference is, I don't.
Down for the count.
What the hell!
Reassuring arms, a kneeling rescuer.
I am a featherweight, lifted,
Uprighted somehow to my feet again.
But I stand shaking. Unsettled.
Hot tears slide unbidden
Down my rug-burned cheeks.

Still held tight, I brush away my tears,
Pick the nearest chair ... let myself sink into it,
Safely fade into its backrest.
I crave, please, no notice.
Yet fastened upon me anyway—
A roomful of eyes, sympathetic, merciful.

———— **Or not.** ————

Tears of humiliation brim again,
But this time, they must not fall.
I grind my thumbnail into my fingertip,
Suck in my breath,
Stare a thousand yards beyond the quavering tears.
HOLD.

And hold they do.

Only then can the fighter in me limp into that ring again.
I work with the crowd for eight hours more;
Gosh dang, my left foot swells and throbs.
What a hard-fought battle with no victory over pain.
My triumph this day, the grit that drives me
To write a couple solid stacks of new contracts.

End of day. My inner fighter rushes me
Straight to the Emergency Room.
"Here for what?" ER Admin asks. *"Foot?"*
Oh, You, with your averted eyes cast down,
Your tone just gave you away,
My inner fighter chides him.
It scoffs next at pain itself. *"Foot sounds silly, even to me."*

Wheeled and secluded behind blessed curtains
—no eyes here.
White-noise silence ... then comfort at last from
Laughter, camaraderie—my girls and me.
How much sweeter the wait now than being alone.

So slick the way the x-ray tech travels to me, click, click.
"Pictures are perfect," Doc proclaims,
"Your foot is broken!" **Broken. Yeah.** Perfect.
Shooed homeward, bobbling along, me,
My big black boot, crutches, 'n the bill. Perfect.

Passing the Admin's desk, I want to lean over and say,
Mr. Admin, say you're sorry ... for doubting me.
I am sorry for doubting myself. So—we're even.
Well, except I have the broken foot and a broken mind.

And even so, my inner fighter 'n me,
A full day of new business,
A throbbing pile of contracts.
Down for the count? **What the hell!**

Admit to the Following

This admission will leave me naked—
If you will shut your ear around my news,
I will *whisper it.*
But it must remain our secret.

Yours and mine.

Look in your rearview mirror—
See that silver-headed woman trailing you?
It is ... a friend ... in need of your help.
She—that is, I, don't mind, slipping along behind,
Arriving second all the time.

Lead me down the streets
I've traveled many times before.
I should know where I am going,
But my mind's no longer mine.
So, please, ease my fall into this new spot,
Second and behind.

Every day, gracefully, you cue me, ensuring
I know what I don't remember.
You smile with love, understanding, and
Patience, mostly.

Such generosity of time.

Make no mistake, I do know
My mental armor suffers daily chinks.
Like the many miles traveled, an old car's rusty
Undercoat begins to show.

It's not that easy, the hiding I do.
But it takes less effort

I feel unkempt, demeaned, undone.
Perhaps, like a homeless broken soul who wanders
The underbelly of my city, Las Vegas?
Comfort her. Comfort me.
We're grateful you've come.

I wonder, though, for her and for me,
Now that we need you,
Is it fair to ask ...
May I be accepted as a child of God?
For times first—I am learning,
You are the backbone of my courage.

Squeeze.

>>LABELED<<

It's not about an enemy invasion
With ground soldiers dodging bullets
LABELED—enemy.

═══════ You die. ═══════

It is a Word War. You are marked, none the less.
Stomped into the medical system
With such furor, danger appears
—and disappears into the miles of files.
Hidden deeper, far under the paper foliage.
Does that mean the terrorist is gone?

No, Memory Soldier.

Listen. I awaken in the wee hours.

What is it I see,
Besides the 2 a.m. clock's face?

I see an enemy of mine—Unruly Mind.
That's what I see
 ...and the infernal marching of time.

What is it I hear?
Am I what they say of me?
Or... am I still the same ol' me?
Why does it matter?
Does it matter?

Oh, it matters what they say!
Diagnosed to the Battlegrounds of A.
The end result is all the same,
No militia needed from outside in
For disappearances hasten from inside out

Hey! Hey!

Remember me, it is my inalienable right!
Stand up. Fight without ravished despair.

"Enemy, don't count me out," **I say**, I say, I say
What's in a label any ol' way?

I'm needed by people

—LABELED people, like me.

Making Sense
of the Senseless

Signs, occurrences, no longer can be ignored.
So I chase down the answers to the unanswerable.

But, diagnosis of dwindling memory comes my way!

Still, I falter in ways to make sense of this.
I can ignore. I can take the meds they recommend.
Neither of which I intend to do.

How do I *make sense of* AD?

I think it is to make a difference ... it is the only way.
Perhaps telling my story, describing fears,
And depicting vulnerability
In a personal log, disclosed and on display.
Uncover my secret—the constant affront—
For all to see.
Step to the side, miss the deep dark hole
In our sidewalk travels—
Don't fall in it, for there is always another way.

If I can make a minute habitable,
Hours manageable and a day gone by ...
Perhaps bring you a smile where one is not,
Show you some light ... **for there is!**

I win—you win—
It's a win-win!

You are not alone—

I'm here to travel and fight our way!
I want to shore up your doubts—
It'll be time well spent—
To be of help and support to you and community.
Leaving a legacy in my years left
To my children and family.
That they may ease into
Whatever lies ahead.
And who knows?
I may be here
For a long
Time.

YES!

T i c k . **T o c k .**

The little hand is at ... four o'clock.
See it move? **I cannot make it stop!**
Like in my half marathon, racing for the finish line,
Brow furrows as I run frantically against time ...

T i c k . **T o c k .**

So it is with the midnight clock viewing,
I grab the little hand,
Stop it from moving.
There. I made time submit.
Does that mean ... time has stopped?

‖ **No,**
‖ **It does not.**

Oh, heebie-jeebie night mind of mine,
Racing to all possible jittery dark places.
Breathe in reason—
Hey, listen, I have questions.

Am I what they say of me?
Or ... am I still the same ol' me?
Why, does it matter? **Oh, it matters!**
So ... if God is in each of us,
Does that mean I am worth saving?

‖ **Maybe not, I think,**
‖ **Ravaged to despair.**

T i c k . **T o c k .** T i c k . **T o c k .**

Finally, I fall to sleep, but soon I stretch,
Yawn, get up, by habit, by faith, bright-eyed.

I plant myself in my smiling, fun-loving facade.
Mornings are my blessing.
Ahhh ... what am I feeling today?

I take heart: **don't count me out!**
What's in a label any ol' way?
I'm needed
By people with people like me.
Let me help, support others—
Don't take me away,
I need my sleep in order to . . . .

Morning, Marathon Runner, T i c k . **T o c k .**

Measured

Houses of ill repute come foreshadowed
In many trappings,
Sheltering and boldly resembling the pimp
Who entices his prey
By filling the needy connection for acceptance,
Initially all hidden agendas—

Soon **stripped** f a r   a n d   a w a y.

Be watchful of the simple acts
When divided and ushered to assigned quarters
By the well-trained choreographed walk,
The non-supple, square-shouldered attendant
To lure us in,
Shred our reluctance,
Disrobe any objections,
=**Strike away at all confidences,**
Down, down to our knees—
Right where they want us to be!

Entŕe
This mortal man chosen by thee
Stagnate in stature,
Symbolizing the high honor and role.
Indubitably, you know the name.
Findings are clear.
Sick—you are.

Just like that

Stripped f a r   a n d   a w a y.

∘∘ CAUGHT ∘∘

Just like many older brothers
Who tattle on their younger sis,
It happened to me
At a young age, just a kid.
He made me squirm so I ran and hid,
Not wanting to be seen.
That feeling holds true still ...
Today.

I utter something twice, thrice—
Let alone my mentioning it yesterday.
What I said and to whom it was said
I cannot say.

Shhhoot! *Maybe you've not noticed*?
Uh-oh. (You did.)
Instantly I go from good to internally forsaken—
And devastated ...
I know it's only my 15-second story to myself, but

I'M FEELING CAUGHT!

Stripped, and ashamed.
Embarrassed.
It's about the fear of being reminded,
Uncovered, disrobed.
Or is it about feeling reprimanded?

Wiping tears inside of me,
I hear my own words say,
"Truly it is."

Hear me now,

"It's not you, you're okay."
As I *hear you, what can you do?*

"Nothing, but make light of it," I whisper.
"For without you, where would I be?
Up that proverbial tree meowing like a scared
Baby kitten, that's where. I love you for trying.

I terribly wish ...
I could love me
... for trying, too!

I *May,* **I May Not**

I *may,* **I may not,**
Have normal time.
Suspicions tell me ...
Connect now, just in case,
Before I may ... **just slip away!**

You might think
How dramatic can she be!
I don't want to hear about her
Preparedness for quiet wilderness!

I say to you
With huggable love
And understanding.
I know. I know.

In life it happens,
My time has come.
To put conviction
Where my mouth once was.

So darn it, somehow ...
It's up to me to show
Will to fight any In-c-o-m-petency.
And **I can ... I will ...** I am.
With my heart in your hand.
It's lucky me.
I'm not so sure about ... lucky you.

But who is to question
A *chartered plan by the Guy Above?*
Does He administer stolen moments,
A year, or five, or twenty-five?

I know not, but think …
It's that we're in the game,
Smiles sometimes hard to find.
So let me cuddle right up next to you on this
Life or death adventure … of the truest kind.

And only with a healthy mind
I hope to stay a long, long time.
Only He knows, if I *may*, **I may not,**
And I know—if not, **please not!**

THE LIGHTER SIDE OF **STRONG**

I am sitting on
THE LIGHTER SIDE OF **STRONG.**
For the most part
Climbing towards solution,

══ **Diminished some.** ══

Join me in my fight.
Knowledge.
Details.

Oh, don't feel sorry!

Let me be patently clear,
"No Pity"
Sign displayed here.
Save it for those more deserving—
Heavier hit, less mobile, cascading in need.

I am
Captive
In your care.
Your concern.
Your love.
And your voices of "Atta girl."

That is all I need.
Well, that
And eat greens, juice, exercise, smile, hug a lot, spread
Joy, Embrace the unembraceable.

When I miss the LIGHTER side of strong
Gently nudge me.
I know better
While I'm ...
In your gentle care.
Wrapped in your concern,
And catching the steadiness of your love,

I feel LIGHTER and LIGHTER—and **STRONG.**

Invisible Three

Doesn't enter our minds
Of anything wrong.
The perfect picture of health
We seem to all be.

Though we hear it spoken,
Disease comes unexpectedly,
I'm a-thinkin' that must mean ... to you.

Certainly not to me!

I'm good—can't you see?
No, really, I'm healthy as can be.

But you!
Don't smile into that mirror
With confidence certain.
See—Wicked Wheat,
Hellacious Carbs and Sugar Sugar—
They are after you.
Like three bullies in a school yard
Fighting to be in charge.

They want to whoop your butt!

Tell me, please, I want
To hear your story
Of sunshine sublime.
Believe me, though,
It makes no never mind.
There's no hiding
Under that Rock of Denial.

Wheat, Carbs, and Sugar,
Our brains' quiet killers,
Are the guys to be
Scared to death of!!
Forever Present, but Silent
Though they may be—
Bullies Three—
Are after you
And after me.

To My Family

I cherish your smiles,
Your impromptu hugs,
Kisses adorned with perks of support,
Explicit private minutiae of your day.

Our moments together showing your light,
Securing times, places, and you ...
Every detail is captured and contained
By the molecules within me.

My drive and focus is to think

Better. Clearer. Longer.

Is to smile genuinely and grasp tightly
Onto the littlest of moments we share.
To retain pieces of air between us,
And the wisps of time around us.
Everything is important.

I don't want to go, **I say, I think,** i mean.
But when the time comes,
What my words and eyes
Can no longer communicate,
My heart knows forever.
Let me soak in your special essence
That you may radiate through my aura
And feel that you are not alone.

Believe in your intuition to guide you,
The unscheduled dust flurry,
The soft breeze at an unusual time,
The light weight on your shoulder for only an instant,

My scent, the notion of me
Joins you as a silent companion
From time ... to sublime time.

You are safe in me.
Until our time stops,
And I believe, beyond,
As long as molecules go on.

Lovingly,
Mom,
Gram,
Grandma,
Grandma No-No
Your friend and on and on

Grounding

It's a simple accident, I say.
For heaven's sake,
It's not about my recall health!
Does everything have to be?

Of course, **Silly You!**

It's not about a pluckier lipstick,
A well-coiffed hairdo, a prettier self.
It is about you, I mean you—
Not the packaging, it's the
Dig deep, deeper than outside attire

Only-you-know-you, **YOU.**

For heaven's sake,
Where do I turn?
God, or Spirit, or Higher Power, above?

I am listening.

Guess I wasn't listening to slow down some.
The fall, my fall, sure did slow me down.
Sure enough!
Adorn me with
A foot rock holding me—
To Mother Earth.

I seem smaller somehow
Little-er.
Less foreboding, if ever, but
Resurfacing with a new level of humbler voice.

No accident is an accident—it is
A tether, teaching us silence and pause.
Listening with a new ear, a grateful eye,
A gentler hand ... and
It is about being true to one's self,
I mean the kinder, gentler, grateful me
Quieting of myself—

Surrender.

The earth shakes
And I hear,
Well, then?

Three Years Ago

Spanish Lessons UNLV.
Conversational?
Heck no. Accredited class.
You. You. And me.
Friends three.

‖ I learned it,
‖ I thought it,
‖ **I got it!**

I went to say those Spanish phrases
Just like my two friends so aptly did.
Only, thoughts trapped in me,
Brain to mouth to words—caught inside,
Like arriving late at airport gate.

Flight gone—departed!

I did not see,
2010. Trouble ahead.

What was to come?

‖ Tiny nudges towards
‖ Keys to the future
‖ Made no sense.
‖ Until one day,
‖ Today.
‖ **I get it.**

I did not know,
But I was chosen
On a path of disconnect.

Why me?
I ask over and over.

There is no answer
I can see.

RED PANTIES

Where **IS** my mind?
At times I feel like a hog-tied
Horsefly being tail-switched
To simply get through each and every long workday!

Whoooa! Buck it up, Girl, face off bravely
To your commitment and your word.
I say ... and I think ... and I pray ... to find a way.
Yet another health problem—
Absolutely positively absurd!

Looming behind me,
I reflect ... two-years-come-July.
Anesthesia? The Heart/Lung Machine?
The question of my Dad's AD? A broken foot?
It's this, that or the other—or all—
Memory is an issue!
It's decidedly relevant to feel as I do.

That something is wrong.
Not quite right. A mystery—
Answers unknown. But for sure I know ...
Hidden, smothered, covered up are perceptions—
They, a bit askew.
Questions I can't remember to answer,
Not to be scoffed.
Hints of awareness of problems ahead
Tightly tucked away in the
Tangles and the jangles of my brain,
Thoughts abstain and refrain.
So how can I work, be active, keep going, be counted as in?
Even when I think I've got it,

Somehow I find myself in a tailspin.
It's elusive—pray tell.

Got it! I got it! I need assistance,
So I call upon Feng Shui.
Yep, wearing RED PANTIES is the solution
—say what you may!

Do laugh, pshaw, snicker a bit.
To think that red most assuredly did
Assist me today, planting a smile,
Just like the face on a kid.
My very own secret—it's delightful fun—
As I forge ahead.
For certain, for sure,
I couldn't have done it alone,
Without the help of ROSY RED.
And those who know not my secret red joy,
But just help me instead,
To my associates and dear friends,
Who stand beside me,
Shouldering my goofs,
Those silently shading my flaws so they do not show,

I say, with a tear in my eye,
THANK YOU *and Amen.*
And, I haven't forgotten, ROSY RED!

LOST!

As I drive...
I know I know this road,
Quickly, though, where am I going?
If I keep on traveling, the destination will surprise me
And just **APPEAR!**
PLEASE, *where are my wheels taking me?*

When I agreed to lead, I knew where to go,
But I'll be doggone if I know
How in this moment to get us there!
While my foot followed my crazy,
Frantic pressure to the gas pedal for logic
Speeding through the not-so-telltale
Streets & businesses—

I couldn't let her know—the unsuspecting car behind.
My mind only checked in long enough to agree.
It's like my mind was frozen on an ice slick,
Sliding away,
Moving but not helping me to know where.
My heart rapidly pumping,
Keeping beat with my stomach
Like on the world's worst roller coaster ride.
My eyes darting desperately for a recognizable
Landmark that keys in our destination.

I *plead, Please, dear Lord, where am I?*
I know this highway. Come auwn, work!!
Suddenly, I was lost and broken
With no time to belabor the despair I felt.
Tires spin,
I need a solution and now!

Should I stop—
Tell her I don't know where I am—
I'm mixed up?

No, keep driving. It'll come, it'll come.

Ahhh, yes, yes, here it is! The turn-off
To Dragon Boat Racing on beautiful Lake Las Vegas.
Thank you, THANK YOU,
And to a beautiful THANK YOU again!

Profoundly Her

My friend—she was **boldly outspoken**
And more so towards the end, if that could possibly be.
There's no time, she insisted.
I gotta say what I'm going to say.
Stage 4, Brain Cancer has come my way.
But don't you worry; **it only thinks it's got me!**

My visiting day came,
The chemo and radiation dawned its darkness,
But a light came to that black wall of hers.
Vacantly radiant, audibly astute, hard in her stand,
Her story—she saw that light and believed

— the cancer was going away!

Stomach distended, laboring to move.
Contrary to what I see, she continues,
Her smile a flag for plucky and perky.
Quite rationally, bravado, the tone,
"It doesn't really matter, you know. I'm living today."

She continued right on ...
"Take our picture!" she commanded.
We laughed, my friend and I.
Heads touching, we listened to **Click! Click!** Click, Click.
As we sat hand in hand, quietly, she shared ...

   "I'm glad you are here,"
   "That's important to me."

As she touched my face, ever so tenderly,
She maintained,

"You're beautiful, so good to see."
"Remember, tomorrow, I may not know you,
But that doesn't really matter," she added,
With a hint of tease, *"Because, you will know me."*

We chuckle again as I say ...
That I'm not all that sure of me.
She squeezed.

With such profound finality,
Her full-of-life gaze burned right through,
Catching me off guard, and said, eye to eye,

"Are you ready to go?"

Stumbling in silence, I got up to hug.
And, we lingered arm in arm.
Then, I wrestled up my crutches,
Deliberately headed for the open-air spaces.
I needed to breathe.
Turning once, I waved "bye" to my friend.
I didn't know it—she was close to her end.
We spent the time she tailored so perfectly,
So private, so personal, and ...
A treasured gift for me to have **forever and ever.**

Glances

Don't sideways glance,
Raise an eyebrow,

Eye contact with a look of WOW!

I see those.

And if in a diminished state today
Ever so slight as it may be, I see
Your **WOWed** facial expression,
Just know it hurts my feelings.
It attacks the confidence
I have left.

No one wants to appear...

Incompetent.
Less than,
Afraid to speak.

However, sometimes,
I am.

Transformation
Is like the struggle of long-time drug addicts
Wherein they think—and I think—
No One Understands
Just how hard it is for them to stay clean.

Okay, now I think
I might have an idea,
Mine to bear—is to seem normal and fine.
I'm trying with dignity

To hold the test of scrutiny
In high abeyance.
(*Maybe being just plain high would make it easier.*)

Your sideways glances
Are my report card
On my being "just fine."

You know I am as I smile.

Am I, *though?*

Alzheimer's Means

Every day
Someone musters up a well-meaning idea,
To ward away the ... the ...
Dear me, what was it I was going to say?

Oh here it is—Let me continue, if I may?
Constant mind blimps. They jab at me
In every which way—a poke, a pinch!

Half an hour ago I wanted to say ... every
Magazine, so many, many books, tell me about

The perfect pill with just the right magic potion or
A cup of coffee is now good, perhaps with abandon.
It's great to down fish and coconut oil, Vitamin D and
Hold friendships close, socialize daily, exercise,
Eat your greens, eat my greens, eat the greens,
Greens will lower the risk of ...

Whaat's the word I want to use?
Give me a minute—or two—as my mind circles
Around—and around—
... and lands elsewhere. **Some damn where!**

Ahh, here it is ... quick! Let me say ... AD.
Damn it! Doesn't make the same sense—don't you see!
It's frustrating, the muddle is not only on the inside,
It's dang nab **inside, outside,** on every side.

Before I forget, I want to share with you ...
A way, they say, to unplaque and untangle,
Those melding things that
Are s-l-o-w-l-y strangling my brain.

Facts written as gospel true—the brain likes novelty.
Brush my teeth or dial the phone ...
With my non-dominant hand.
How about showering with my eyes closed—
Drop the soap, and find it.
A diagnosed person's version of Hide and Seek.

‖ Tap on a piano ...
‖ Speak a new language ...

I can't even speak my own, dear me!

‖ Be sure and get sufficient REM sleep—

Ahhh, now there is one, right now it's 4:15 ayem!

Constantly shore up defenses of cognitive decline.
Oh, yeah, the funny thing? I do each one of these
But I truly hope they don't ask me to
Chugalug slimy slick
Oyster creatures from the sea.

Because, of darn course, I would!

In Faith's Hands

I'm weary with my health struggles.
Chains that individually imprison me.
Trapped feelings—

Sick to the bone news,
Mad as a hooked fish,
Time-sucking inconveniences—
Time I may no longer have,
Doctors multiplied by a ton, it seems,
Outrageous expenditures—
Medical funds gulped down to zero, past none.

Where did I come from and where am I going?

From rooster's first crow of the morning,
Cock-A-Doodle-Doo!
"Get it up! Get it going! It's morning! It's morning!"
As it comes to me ... Oh, come with me.

HaveFaith-A - D o o d l e - D o o !

In Faith's hands ...

Roams the toggle switch
"I can."

Faith's hands ...

Shores up the pillars
Of human-ness traveled, I need to be
Not alone, but linked together,
United—as a block of steel—
Unformidable. Oh, come with me.

In Faith's hands ...

Fortunes are made.
Illness dazes and fades—in Faith's hands.
Half-full—glass wins awards—in them.
I will switch my mood, move front room
Furniture—celebrate in them.
Soak in bright sunlight—feelings of
Well-being comforted by them.

Breathe faith in—Visualize it—Faith—Say it—
"I AM Faith!"

I AM Faith - A - D o o d l e - D o o !

I know. **I know**. I know. I'm In Faith's Hands.

Driving

I fear I am not in control,
Not always driving with my mind
On the road.
When in, I am mindful and intentional.

As a busy adult, today I find
My workdays filled multi-tasking.
Scurrying car-bound
People waiting,
Got to **get here, there,** everywhere.
Lest business steers another away.

When I'm focused elsewhere, I am out.
As though the conscious mind drives away,
Unmanageable. Cannot comprehend.
The brain is simply out.

Hold it! Wait!

Brakes slammed, a hard left turn.
Flipped a quick ooou'eee!
As though cold water hit my face ...
Mind back on the road, awake again!
Pink-cheeked, scared to attention,
Eyes scanned around, to see who saw ... me.

My mind was ... where?

On an auto vacation.
No on gas pedal starts and sudden stops ...
Reality—it brought me back "in" again.

Shameful,
The rush all out of me.
Instant promise made,
Stay in control of your auto-machine,
You with your Hands on the **Wheel!**
Concentrate.

Shhh, don't tell.
I will. Someday.
But not just yet, not today.
This happens to everyone from time to time.

Doesn't it?

Acceptance of the **Dark Echoes**

I can see I'm not looking so good
As I scrutinize myself
In the magnifying mirror today.

Baggy eyes, rubbed red,
Runny nose and purple skin,

Even when I try to smile,
The lines don't lift.
This face I'm wearing
Is no mask at all.

Setting the mirror aside,
With no further need to reinforce
Sorrowful long days and longer nights.
My torso weighs heavy; I cannot seem
To shore up my shoulder blades.

A longtime dearly cherished friend
Got a mother's worst-feared words,
Your daughter is dead.

*And she ended her life,
By her very own hand.*

My second encounter,
Following too soon after my first.
Another dear friend—
News of her son.
He found no way to proclaim his burden

**Except to end his life in deadly violence,
By his very own hand.**

My throat tightens with a scream
From within, too deep to voice,

No, not her! No, not him!

My question ...*Why? Oh, why?*

These mothers so dear,
My chosen sisters,
My partners in joy.
And now, in grief and despair.

I know I am a million miles outside;
That my sister-friends are understandably
More wrecked than I.
Yet, I, too, am broken enough to understand
That I, and they, will never, ever
Understand the why.

FRIEND

A friend
Is a friend
When ...
She does
What she can.
Even if
She personally feels
It's against her sidekick's
Best interest

And without a win-win.

Putting another
First
Without
Judgment
Or grist
Is
The Ultimate

FRIENDSHIP.

Healthy times
And times not so.
A true friend
Stands strong
And vigilant.
Listens with two ears,
Shares facts with care—
A trusted ally—

One you can depend on.

Through tears of sympathy,
Daydreaming
Over glasses of wine,
Lamenting over
Yesterday's traffic fine.
No matter.
A cherished friend
Shoulders the journey.

So ... *thank you,*

True F R I E N D .

Your loving kindness begets
My humble gratitude.

45 Days In

What if…?
Could it be?
All this worry for naught?

Hmmm, **let's see!**
Doctors **One, Two,** Three,
First two say, "Yes."
Third says, "We'll see."

Doc Number Two, I query,
Have you given me a wrong diagnosis?
Are you positively sure … *it's* AD?

I caution you, **Don't rush to assumption!**

If there is a shred of doubt,
Be certain, be sure.

Put a lock on your throat 'til then,
La la la ARE YOU SURE I HAVE ALZHEIMER'S?
MyMY heart's sitting on what you say.

From your lips to my ears,
"Your brain looks good for your age."

Instantly I brighten in some way,
Possibly be given a reprieve?

Amazing how one little doubt
Brings light to my sphere
Like a lonely bug drawn to the one
Lighted bulb in a frenzied fear.

Hold it, **wait!** *Why … the prescription note pad?*

"I want you to start Aricept immediately. Today."
Fuming inside out, red ears and lashing tongue,
I don't believe in you, Doc Number Two!
No drugs. Not today.

I accept the words of unrest.
Open for all to dissect.
Throw away the prescription note pad
For my mind-altering drugs!
It's way too soon to discuss.
For once on that path—**It's death!**

Until proof shows its hand,
Push, "Celebration"
By Kool & The Gang
I'll stroll to the music,
And sing myself free.

Above Beyond

Take me to the mountains high.
Across the tree tops
Afloat in the sky.
Elevated.

Above all destiny
Where courage is free
Missing—all human debris,
Thinking unlimited-ly.

Sky where sun smiles
And trust is revered,
Warm hearts—indeed—
Universal-ly.

Higher, yet quieter,
Deeper, for sure.
Mission clear.
Imminent.

Write. Share.
Bare my soul.
Help someone—
Indeed I shall.

Until I can't
No more.

Doctors, Doctors

I come to your office,
Stark room, white coats,
Unsure and afraid.
You enter, your eyes askew
Never quite looking
But somehow, you see ... *me?*

Look, Lookie here—it's me.
I come to you in good faith
All dressed nice and neat.
A simple lady looking for a simple answer ...
Just wondering where my memory went.
You say, by tests of elimination
For 70 years old—I'm looking darn good,
But, yep, **you have the A!**
Take these—you'll be fine
For another day.

Well, wait, what happened here!

A minute ago I was just fine.
Now I need to swallow these.
Could you, please, for me, define?

Crazy I think I'd be
To cave right in at first-see,
So let's get some law and order—here and now.
And ask, what happened to the Process of Elimination
To substantiate the title of AD?

The articles I read say to hold up on the drugs;
The outcome of benefits to patient is inconclusive.
Did you hear? Do you care?

I feel my tests are inconclusive.
And yet ...
It is drugs you are practicing,
You are running a patient numbers game.
Not unlike the pimp who runs his
Girls of the night for profit,
You run your patients of the day,
Getting us hooked on the idea drugs are the only way.

Finding me scared and weak as your prey,
I find the medical system failing its patients.
And Big Pharma ... well, they are the Big Guns.
And the doctors ... well, the doctors ... *well?*

The Weight of Waiting

Not for the first time,
Or for the second,
Here we are, arm in arm,
Jenn and I, seated in
A personality-sterile office,
Unwelcoming chairs,
25 peeps—every seat full.
Like a room full of sitting ducks ... waiting, waiting,
Anticipating ... *the shot and the pluck*!

My jaw grows tight; I begrudge minutes
Waiting—**I think we should leave!**
But hold it ... reality is
I wanna know the score. The blasted test results.
I hug Jenn's arm—we cuddle closer.

Waiting still, one hour passed ... staff lunch arrives,
Smells waft under doorways, through hallways.
Nose knows—it's an Office Pizza Invasion.
Everyone invited ... except those waiting twenty-five.
What is your thinking, *People in White*?
That I can't—your patients can't–*smell*?
Won't remember? We're all still waiting.
One hour and a half by now.
Waiting!
And they know it.

HOW *is it your time is more important than ours*?
I'm here to see if my mind isn't quite clear.
But to Acts of Kindness—or insensitivity—
I am well aware.

Office courtesies, niceties—**missed your front door!**

Two and one-half hours elapse.
Waiting game over as doctor and staff,
Stomachs full, return to patients.
Now, yes, doctor delivers his news.

Oooh no.
A confirmation we desperately do not want to hear.

I sigh. Heave a ho. And another.
I take a minute to collect myself,
Then I draw from within.
I am surprised
How much stronger my hope is than my fear.

Wham Bam!
You offer me a third opinion—
Now I offer you mine:
No, sir.

PERSEVERANCE

I am not afraid to die, **just not anxious to stop living!**
That makes me like half the seniors
Plodding around in health alternatives.

Today, I heard about ... yet another memory test—
Helps paint the picture of murky brain functions.
My thought—*Why rush?*
First response, I am going to pretend I didn't know of it.

It's a given I'm sitting at denial's front door, but . . .

Second contemplation,
I grab my big-girl panties and pull for dear life.
Cinch my belt tight as though
Fearful I'll lose a body part.
Withering weight-wise, facial lines ingrained,
My insides screaming at me—I want to shove this aside!
A mere notice—as I push the gas pedal down and drive.
I zip through the lights, forging ahead.
THIS would be the usual time ... to get lost instead.

The bought-and-paid-for spindly sticks ever-ready beside me
Then, too, I'll lug the boastful and pretentious
One-hundred-pounder—weighted broken-foot boot
All so I can go someplace I don't want to go,
Hearing something I am not sure I want to hear.
Ahhh, here I am all the same.
I park. **I sit**. I breathe.

Deeply appreciative, I am able to plod forward,
I drag through the parking lot like
I am in a field of muddy quicksand.
Cumbersome crutches, and purse in tow, both hands

Maneuvering me firmly in a bended-straight stance,
My nose runs like an open faucet—allergies
I add to the mix of demands—
To find a Kleenex takes my immediate
Attention and full command.
I stop and gratefully balance with a shaky
One-footed halt—ahhh, the tissue.
Alone and lower than ever before in life, I proceed humbly,

Plastering my remember-to-smile face in place.
I feel very much like a bag lady, unable to carry her own bag.
Hoping that person, yes, you at the door,
Will you hold it, pretty please?

Here I am tired, wore out, not supposed to eat sweets—**but I do!**
Manage grabbing a big chocolate cookie, and water, too.
A gracious volunteer comes to my rescue,
I feel hugged by an angel.
Why was I here? Oh, yes.
This test could be an opportunity for me and for others...
But I'm beginning to hate the thought of a memory challenge—

At Cleveland Clinic, masterfully the test score reads—
I don't fit the guidelines for this particular blind study.
Don't know why I want to cry—
This is good news for heaven's sake!!

I gather my things to retrace my steps,
Hailed from a-far, "Would you like your picture taken?"
A kind gift offer, I know, but sheer exhaustion gives way to
A slight smile, hand waive and nod that indicates, no more.
I bow my tear-ridden face and wipe the droplets on my sleeve
Never before feeling this grab-for-my-life total disrepair.

God, are you here? Can you get me home?
Please, pretty please.

Mind Less

Every day
Someone musters up a well-meaning idea,
To ward away the … the …?
Damn these constant mind blimps.

Dear me, what was it I was going to say?
Oh here it is—*I'll continue, if I may?*

Your kindness of finishing my sentences—
Your look of … *well?*
Or one of emotional pity,
Strains the patience each of us experiences,
Creating tiny jabs, a poke, a pinch, in every which way.
Eroding my confidence.
Wearing on nerves, like a jacket too tightly fit.

How to fight through to solution,
Not diminishing the us in you and me?
My promise to you is …
I'll fight for awareness, to be understood.
And your part is to get that.
I am forever caught in … *whaat's the word I want to use?*

So be patient and give me a minute or
Two as my mind circles
In and around …
… and lands over there.

Some damn where!

THE PARTY

I accept the invite
Gladly.
To be included
Feels so familiar-ly good.

And then
Doubt pops up
Its tiring head ...
Was I invited
Because I was on
The A List

Or ... *because?*

Internally
Addressed and redressed,
I choose
The road
It Doesn't Matter.

My car door slams
In front of the party house.
With gala anticipation
I don
My merrymaking smile,
Climbing high as though rock climbing for
My attitude to match, yelling—

I'm excited! I'm excited! I'm excited!

And, therefore, I am.

I enter the doorway,

Brightly lit for the evening guests,
And commence to mingle and
Catch up with old friends, meeting new ones,
Chat,
Exchange,
Listen,
And I truly loved the evening.

Thank you for inviting me.

I.SAW.ME

I sit, reticent and quiet
In a doctor's office soft chair,
Curious about others coming and going
When enters a man and his wife.
She was hunched over, following, not really there.
They settle directly across from me.

I try to refocus on my magazine article,
But in one ear, softly overhear,
"Why am I here?" from her lost face
And blank stare to her obviously armored husband's ear.
"We're visiting," he quietly says, no smile, anywhere,
Not even an eye, giving her grace.
So I do—though perhaps not my place.

"Wh-ere?" slowly articulated in two syllables, she asks.
"Doctor's office. We're visiting here,"
Keeping his newspaper held tight.
I wonder how hard this is for him. I guess, very hard.
For sure, I know it is captivatingly difficult
For me to watch and hear.
Like overhearing a family feud,
Knowing I have no business listening.

"I don't want to be here,"
She mimics and nudges forward, nearer to him.
Silence reigns supreme.
No motion he makes to comfort her.
Then, she tentatively looks up at him
And snuggles in under his arm,
And inquires one more time, *"Why are we here?"*

I imagine he dreads, as much as she, this office visit.

Why else would he casually answer her
Without even a look up?
"Just for a few minutes," were the words he could spare.

"I don't want to be here," she repeats her thought.

Not tuning in,
Nor eyes that leave his news print yet, he says,
"Ummm, I know."
A tired man, his look of resignation burns deep
The pages he probably doesn't see.
Every motion of his body reeks, perfunctory.
I pretend I do not see. But I do.
I feel sorry for him.
Or should I want to shake him, I ask myself.

Who am I saddest for … him, her, or me?
I can't help but wonder …

Who will be sitting on that weathered
Red-leather couch—with me?

I am sure it will be someone who will stop, look,
And listen to me as though I matter.

Suddenly, I get up to leave—I am ready to go—
Even though this is my very favorite doctor of all.
And that is saying one heck of a lot, you know.

As I hear, "Hello, Nancy. Come right in."

Luckier Than Most

In the time
Since getting my news,
Not any words
One wants to hear ...

I've read, I've asked, I've researched.

My echo, *"This cannot be!"*
I felt the resounding horror
... of what comes next.
But, hey, there are so many worse off
... than me.

There are the sick and lonely,
Moving around the streets, unprotected.
Or addicts, unable to say no.
Suicides as a chosen end
To struggling day in, day out.

And then—just look at me—
I'm seventy.
I'm nestled in support.
I'm hopeful in faith.
And now I understand
It's not so hard ...
To be diagnosed with A.

Still, how do I make sense of this?

I think to make a difference ... is the only way.
Perhaps telling my story, my fears and my sins,
In a personal log, disclosed and on display.

If I can make a minute plausible,
Hours manageable and a day gone by ...
Perhaps bring you a smile where one is not,
Show you some light ... **for there is!**

I win—you win—it's a win-win!

I want to do that—it'll be time well-spent—
To be of help and support to community,
Leaving a legacy in my years left,
Somehow, someway.

Dancing
THROUGH THE DAFFODILS

Yellow is my favorite color.
It makes me happy like no other.
It makes me think life is good.
And be that, it should.
It makes me feel the brightness,
Wearing a crown like a fairy princess.
It makes me glad to be alive
Even with life's ups and downs,

I'm happy to survive!

This is my life!

I create from it what I will.
It is up to me to find the good.
And ... expand on that.

I dare you, Dancing Yellow Seeker!

"Have a daffodilly day!"

DrugPartners

Well-coiffed
And greeting me
With reserved but polite
Formality fitting his position
And title is Dr. MD.

> Body language
> Leaves nothing
> To be
> Misinterpreted.

I believe words have **POWER**
When they are used
By doctors starched and in white,
And backed by the unseen
Pharma Gods
Issuing their
Laundry list of drugs to entice.

I demand to know–
What makes you so sure your
Prescribed drugs are the only way?
Do they give me a fighting chance?
Or is the important part
A financial advance?

Left with that!
I—the patient—
Must figure it out.
Do my homework.
Leave it not only to those
Who think they are in charge,

But grab myself to reality. Belly up to the bar,
For it's my disquieting body, **not theirs!**

Anger strikes me fightin' mad.
I want to kick some doors down!
Stop 'em in their tracks—
The Pharmaceutical Bandits.
And doctors, too.
Are you potentially killing me
With your prescription pads?

Be awake, I say.
Be present.
Learn & Decide.
Sure, sometimes I must agree,
Say yes to drugs,
Thankfully.

But I want to be an informed
Consultant,
And Third Partner
In the decision of what I take!

HAIKU

It's my birthday!
It's my birthday!
Hold your guns, you young lady, you
... it's NOT today. Coming up,
Soon it will be.

I have packages—*three*.
Beautifully wrapped in
torn, colorful paper.

I know, I know.

Decorated especially just for me.
My skin crinkles
With anticipation for what's inside.
My cousin created surprises for me
To see. **W h o o o o o e e e.**

I'm watching them,
These mysterious boxes
Sitting on my counter top
Enticing my curiosity.
Smiles and giggles bubbling
All the way through me.

I hold one, inspect the corners.
Then another, precise as can be.
So tantalizing—the process of discovery.

Open them now!
Then where would I be?
I twitch, I turn. I squirm. Ahhh...
What could it hurt?

Sooo, I decide to unhinge
One little end of one—
The smallest square of the three.
Ooops, I can see the fun oozing out the corner.
So quickly, I snap the wrapping back ...
Shut. Flawlessly. There, perfect.
Redone. What fun!

It's for another day.
I so love the chase and the wonder
Of packages one and two and three.

A day or two passes,
The birthday presents grabbing out to me,
They really did.
Today the time has come.
I grab up the smallest delight.
Disrobing it, slowly, tenderly,
Like uncovering a newborn baby's bum
... for the first time.

I slide out the black box.
Enthralled, I read

HAIKU

And immediately I know
The treasure bestowed upon me.

From my
Cousin,
My
Friend.

Mind-Boggling Networking

You have no idea

> The time ...
> The energy ...
> The perseverance ...

It takes me.

Scan, copy, title, and email,
Time and again.
It goes through in my mind,
Step **One**, **Two**, Four,
Hit Send button.

No! Shoot! Or is it a Shit, oh dear!

I missed Step Three.

A single ten-minute mission
Takes me an hour ... or more.

Phone rings, emails return,
Several reminders—I missed one page.
I sigh ... and begin again.

So, beloved networking friends,
I attend before you,
Feeling undressed.

I find myself in the position of
A woman whose mind was once sharp,
But knowing now, it is not.
Not even my clothes feel the same.

I used to wear clothes pulled from my closet
Looking fit for a challenge, I thought.

Today? My mirror sees a heavily burdened woman.
It pulls and pushes to manage the extra stress I see,
From stretched muffin-top seams to the look of weary.

Disgruntled. I attend my Wednesday-morning meeting.
Weekly, it takes chutzpah, gumption, and resolve!

So I will my assigned secretary load to seem "normal,"
But I cry from inside,
What you see is the mind-boggling networker.
That smile you compliment me on every week?
Is inwardly turned upside down,
A frightened new true me.
I ask for your encouragement here.
How else can I display qualities I'm struggling to possess?
Like a mime whose smile is painted on,
Her mind focused elsewhere.

It's okay, you're all right, I say to myself.
After all ... hours-long heart surgery, prolonged
Anesthesia, all take their toll. I suffer the marks.
As though that's not enough, my brain takes
Another hit, furthering the darkness.

Yet my heart opens as never before.
It must seek, and it will find,
What more and more I need—
Your generous lights to guide me.

I See

I see the fear in your eyes, which deepens
With each memory indiscretion,
Appointment missed,
Recall unattained,
Blank look returned 'cause I don't get what you say.
You mention I missed a text.

Didn't I see it? You called me, too?

My stomach sinks. I'm reticent.
I didn't sign up for this—for me or for you—
It's hurtful in so many ways.

*Would it have been easier for you if
I'd spared the grim details?*

My guess now is yes. My eyes fill.
I simply didn't know how to
Weather the unknown future ahead—for us.
How to prepare you if it's not for
Openness between us players
—you, my loving family, my fabulous friends, *and me?*

Much like the moves on a chess board,
Calculated and thought-provoking,
This life game is about shifting
Strategies overshadowed by the ugliness
Of a hostile memory takeover.
Recognition squeezed to submission until body
Compromises to the final end.

Oh, this is more than you signed up for?

Me, too, my darlings, me too—and way more.
Not often will one find the test of a disease asked for.
It fastens itself, unseen, and those affected must cope.
I wanted to make this process easier for you, not harder.
I would hold the hurt if I could,
Shelter your heart and make your tears into sunshine.

Oh my gosh, if only I could. **I would, I would,** I would.
I'd hug you and fill you with all the
Love your body could hold,
Make you strong, knowing you
Have the best parts of me and will
Live happily ever after—forever ...

What if . . .

Words I want to hear ... I hear.
Maybe I don't have what it is they say I have.

I'm excited. Delighted. Thrilled. Ecstatic.

—*What if. . .*
It's a Wrong Diagnosis?

Doc No. 3, could this be?
Exploring, eye to eye—
 "Yes," his words halted, his mouth shrugged,
"Maybe not, you are far too clear-headed."

OMG, Golly Gee!
What if the void
That's been before me
Is now diminished
More than somewhat
By a ...

—*What if. . .*
Eating, praying, crying, laughing-
Perhaps by wearing purple, green,
And pink together on a Tuesday morning!
By being proactive and fighting as hard as I know I can
Gets me back to Square One
With normal people—**Disease free!**

—*What if. . .*

Dilemma

It feels like my friends
Are beginning to pull away.
I *think*
They don't know what to say.

Are my mind warps—
The deteriorating truth—
Too difficult to be around?

The elephant suddenly too
Big for the roooom?

No one likes
Uncomfortable.

Or is it simply an outside

|| Image of the smiling
|| Running,
|| Laughing

Buddy—
Who doesn't show up
To play in the same way?
They wonder …
But cannot say …
Where are you today?

Then there's …
It may all be misconcocted
In my own quacky mind.
How do I extract the accuracy?
I listen with my eyes as I
Fight with my resolve to keep

Present,
In touch,
Together,
Connected.
"Slow down,"
My friends would say.

Then again, other times
I'm quite sure...
THIS IS my
Pesky Monkey Mind,
My Unruly Censor,
My own story stuff,
Busy as can be!

Without asking, for truly the words
Will not pass through stiffened lips,
Dear hearts, am I out of sync? Does it feel
To you that I'm really pulling away to
The awkward place called A?

Long ago when I was little,
My mom used to say,
"Be seen and not heard."
And here I am today
Feeling just that way!
A slow learner, she might be
Thinking from Above.

Please don't go away.
Your job, my collaborators,
Should you be willing to accept it,
Is to know you're doing all you can.

And, I know it, too!

A New Love Calls

My spirit
Tugs intently
Like an untethered soul
Wanting to escape
The mundane activities of daily working.

Explaining reports to one employee after another
A broadcast of the multi-faceted informational changes
Igniting many inconsistencies and my insecurities—
Until I can hardly speak.

Go away,
You pesky thoughts, you,
As the busy-ness pushes
The elements of discontent into line.
No matter that it's the 1,000th meeting—
It's where vocabulary, rules and regs define,
Challenges to both sides.
Professionalism standing firm,
The questions answered hold
Truth but no longer any joy.

Another day, like many
When restless misgivings
Call louder than the hushes
Can stop the in-house roar.
Is it time?

Escaping through a side entry
At midday break,
A moment to collect
And wrestle with restrain.

The **kerplunk** of the heavy door, closed,
Dividing me in two;
One side comfortable with the old,
The other, well, unleashing inspiration brand new.

The feeling, it's safe here outside,
I lean up against the building's
Bristly surface which feels like
An unshaven man's sharp whiskers
Upon my open palms—noted—
But holds my body stable and erect.
Head touches, chin aiming upwards,
Heat of the sun washes away the smell of auto-oily air,
But no never mind, my eye lids relax and shut—
For just a moment—I *promise myself*.
A reprieve.

Breathe in ... and out ... and slowly then
Lost is the franticness of rushing.

Ahhh,
The breeze runs across my tired face
And a smile appears,
Leaving its stamp of upturned
Delight.
Taking me back to my cozy place—
A special hideaway from childhood.

Envision, salty breeze turns magical
And takes me back many years
Where sea gulls squawk
Unmercifully, yet with an abandon
Espousing freedom and liberty, joy.
I love that place where I first
Recognized there was new world possibilities
Which lay just beyond my grasp.

My desire for more had to be fulfilled.
It was then and... so it is now.

Suddenly,
Eyes open as my body moves
From the building's no-longer-needed embrace.
It's been good to me, my chosen vocation, but
I've received my retirement permission slip.

Renewed and with confidence,
The asked question has an answer—
Yes, yes, and yes—this is the end.

I'm excited and ready to blaze a new frontier.
New calling, **here I am!**

Roadmap To *Happiness*

Turtles are **s l o w**
That's for sure—we know.
Don't doubt their managing
To get to their goal, though.
So it is with me.
I may be **s l o w**
But hey, I'll get to my destination

Mmmmmmmy way!

I **love** turtles
And the lesson very well may be

Stop! Enjoy the journey!

To hell with the A.

Mother's Word

So help me, I'm beginning to feel
More and more like a disappearing
Chambermaid who slips
In and out of rooms unnoticed.

I ask the Universe with tempered confidence,
Adopting a formal tone, *So, what is next?*
Shall I ask for help to move through
My fear of being seen, but not heard—
Or stay silent—*so not to bother?*

I wonder and I worry ... if there is an answer,
Please, please, may I hear?

Mother used to tell me—
"Get up. Clean up. You'll feel better."
And I did.
Still do.

I manage first by getting out of bed and showering;
The warm water glides, seeks, nurtures.
Next, a large amount of creamy coconut oil
Fades away over my inviting body,
Cures on so many levels.
Choose an outfit—my best color, blue—
And adorn myself from head ... to matching shoe.
Emulating a lady of my age and stature
But, of course—that's true.
Hair the shade of snow, it'll have to do.
I pat on barely a dab of face color, light blush-n-glow,
And eyebrows darkened
Just enough to show I'm still here.
I trust no one will notice ...
My delicate eyelids are drooping.

I'll camouflage them with a big irresistible smile
Which spreads—at least for an ample mile,
That thankful smile.

I say, as I admire, "Mirror, Mirror, on the wall,
Who is the fairest of them all?"

After scrutinizing the reflection—I sneak a quick wink!
Satisfied, it is indeed work completed
By an artist's hand
And nothing short of facial-sculpted perfection covers
The weathering of a full life span.

Looking skyward, **"Mom, I'm ready to go!"**

Matriarch

It all began with maternal architecture,
A tall statuesque Las Vegas building
With many useful years behind her.
She's loved, nurtured, and respected.

With the worn edge of endurance,
Her facade and infrastructure
Begins to chip and undo.
Today, she is in need of repair.
It is time for her progeny to take over—
The maintenance and the care.

Liken this strong mature building
To the Matriarch of the Nelson Family.
She watches her structural offspring
As they claim their personal radiance.
Core construction, family-building,
Yet each block uniquely different from another.
Built to brainstorm brilliant ideas
With catchiness of reason.
Perform creative skyline imagination,
Revered in well-labeled professionalism,
Stand integrity tall with honest acclaim,
Shoulder stronger for longer than she—
All worries and flurries
Of everyday wear and tear.

To relinquish her stoic stature—let her
Miracles—absolutely you, and you, and you—
Carry on as she knows each one of you will do.
One of the warm glows from Above that comforts you
And the shadow you see here and there,
Is her loving-kindness walking with you ...
Proud for you to be her maternal heir.

I'm excited!
I'm excited!
I'm excited!

Grab onto
A new bold
Unknown
Future
Helping,
Supporting,
Nurturing
Others
Bruised by the
Diagnosis of Disease,
Struck hard by illness,
Devastated by Dementia,
Alzheimer's or
Plain old Depression.

Living a life of excellence and integrity.

Breathe in to full lung capacity.
Hold it. Listen.
Breathe taller.
Set an intention.
Live greater and grander.

Live my life today allowing someone else to win.

Let's gather together,
Combine strengths,
Collect laughter.
Prepare and walk
Touching hearts and hands.

None of us got to where we are today alone.

Let's build a fortress,
Connect
Unite.
I am excited.
We are.

A Stamp of Love

Stamps, colorfully adhered, intricately designed,
Positioned like puzzle pieces licked in place.
Panoramic in stature, artistic in value,
From a Peace Bridge 1927-77 USA,
To an International Women's Year USA,
A whole year commemorating us girls—I like that.
Another, Gold Star Mothers USA worthy of 3 cents,

I cannot help but wonder—only 3 cents?

But come to the rescue, I find that in days back when,
First class postage was only
3 cents and now I like that then.

Two large, oblong stamps named,
Letters—mingled souls, 10cUS each
I like we are **connected–forever–wherever** we are.

Standing last, but certainly not least, in a decorative line
Is a *Purple Heart Forever Stamp*
Trimmed in memorable gold.
No monies stated for no earthly
Amount would be enough.
It calls for a moment of silence,
And deep-rendering appreciation.
Thank you, Soldiers, for all that you've done.
It's not enough to say you are heroes and the reason our
American home shores are safer; but, you are—
And we are.

Postage positioned precisely, with intent, and by design,
Holding banner headline above black-markered
Hand-printed address

Zip-coded, including last four numbers—

First time I'd seen!

Stuffed with poems of work critiqued
By my cousin's eagle eye,
Securely tucked in a highly decorated
Envelope mailed by the
Hubby-of-her-lifetime—
Both holding my title of ... *Crème de la Crèmes.*

Instilling feelings of warmth, trust,
And treasured love renewed
With each and every incoming postal
Gift of unlimited value.

It doesn't get better than that!!

I *feel* Your Love

How do I hone my skills,
Sharpen my mind?
Stay in step toe to toe
With the universe's wishes?
Listen more intently, answer
Quicker, speedier, better,
Maybe even have a chit-chat
Tongue-in-cheek, with you?
Laughing and
Conversing and keeping myself
In a razor-sharp cutting edge
Conversation, or two?

How? **I do not know.**

A knife grinder who makes his living
At sharpening things, can he
Make my
Monosyllabic responses
Occur less and less?
Cut away at the part of my brain
That does not work so mighty fine?
The doctors—can they?
Scientists? Just wishing for it?

No, to all.

Between momentary
Uplifts of the mom,
Grandmother, friend,
You all once knew—
You need to know
There is no relief today.

But, it's coming, they say.

Oh, I know, my loves,
You are having to cope
With all of my changes, too.
With each reminder of
My flat lackluster look,
Emotionless face,
If even for a brief moment—
I know it casts an uncomfortable
Burden upon you.

Will it help to know? ...

You make me warm inside and I feel loved.
That helps me. I hope it helps you, too.

Grandchildren's Bargain

Brayden, Delaney, Rachel Anne, Jack

Four young'uns making a difference in a world
Of fractured meaning, unresolved solutions,
And opportunities abound.

Use your noggin, grab your diplomas along
With your nurtured assurance and pin it to you
Like an athlete's name is sewn on a letterman's sweater.
Tightly. Never to be dismissed or removed.

Cherish Forever.

Just like our laughs, giggles, and tingly tingles
Hold in you deep down,
Keep in a locked compartment,
Close to your heart, unchangeable.

Cherish Forever.

Let's make a pact, a bargain
Between the two's of us ...
Four times over.
None of us are to look backwards
Filled with regrets or if-onlys.
Let's be forward-focused and knowing
We've done the best we can—in the moments we've had.

Please hold onto ...
When the time comes and you look into my eyes
And my adoration is locked inside, unable to be seen,
No worries, no worries.

Recall the days back when ...
You saw my smile, felt the warmth from my hugs, and
You heard me say ... *I love you*.

If ever any answers to your questions
Become intertwined in my corrupted mind,
Cannot find their way to my lips,
But only to my clenched fist,
As my dad's did to mine, don't do as I did.
Don't worry, don't worry. *I love you*.

If ever my current words sting for minutes, hurt,
Slap at your kindness and pinch your sensibilities,
Put your tongue to the roof of your mouth, hold tight.
Don't you worry, please don't. *I love you*.

Know that every fiber in my tattered defenses
Will be fighting to hold onto you.
My consolation will be that you know the battle
Against wordless frustrated anger
Is sent from who I've become.
Not from who I am—your Grandma,
Grandma No-No, Gram.

Remain lodged and instilled in our bargain ...
March ahead—we'll be hand in hand.
No worries, no worries.

I am here, feel the stitching around
Your name and my heart... and ...

I love you.

Quiet Approach

Along the Oregon beaches
I walk close to water's edge.
Look to overhead seagull's wings
Flapping in folly and breeze.
Wait! Look, look over there—
Water without an end.

The wind follows the shoreline,
Seaweed stranglers and reeds a-waving hello.
I accept their simple gestures and quiet approach
To catch my eye.

To fluttering sounds, I look,
Birds of feather that flock side by side.
Understand some to be dirty and some playful pests,
But hearing that and seeing them—
They don't seem different somehow.

I like them all...along the beachy shore—
It makes life connect.
Like two older birds, nestled together,
Tweedling, touching.
Beautifully preening themselves, and each to the other.
Adversely, unlike disgruntled pigeon-types,
Making their mess,
Hovering on rooftops and landing too close for comfort,
Together in flocks and rarely separate, alone.
Yin Yang. Perfect harmony within multiplicity.
Otherwise, the world would tilt,
And we'd all be crowded up in one corner.

Let's coalesce—together.
Focus on beauty and calm, leftover refuge.

And focus on wellness, not illness.
Contain those doses of unhealthy realities,
Follow them up by taking a breath of gentle okay-ness.

Create ... the feeling, be aware and safe.
Me too, I am safe, secure.
Challenged, me and you
But in God's good grace.

Changing ◄──► Directions

I am alone. Who cares
That I look through guarded glasses,
Breathe heavily, and stand alone?
Of course, you, and those who care about me.
Others? Maybe none.
But experience has taught me, if nothing changes,
Then, well, nothing changes—
Alas ... let me transform.

Love differently than most do.
Love with abandon
Like a kite catching the last swift wind of daylight,
Up, up, and up, running, shouting, laughing,
Unattached to the outcome.

I know I must forgive righteous indignation—
Of my own expectations.

It's okay to discern with inner awareness of my
Own wisdom dawned,
And careful acceptance of what I see.
In today's world, always discern.

To self I say ... unlock the door to adventure, eye the
Skydivers, hike to the bottom of the Grand Canyon,
And back again,
Or build a church in ... *where-was-that now*?

Seek knowledge, folk and lore, old-time tales
Making body parts stir. **Yes!**
Shiver me timbers.
Think back to 1718, where the swashbuckling
Buccaneer Blackbeard was beheaded,
And his body thrown overboard.

Legend has it that the head circled the
Ship three times before sinking.

I declare!

Get Love Happy. There is no perfect way,
So let me be open to
Finding happiness in all encounters,
Whether by book on the high seas
Or walking the multi-dimensional
Nevada desertscape, attending the
Smith Center for an evening of theatre,
Book club, writer's group,
Plant tomatoes for the first time at 70,
Celebrate birthdays and holidays ...

God's footprints alongside of me mean ...

I am not alone.

SEVEN MONTHS IN
After Diagnosis of A

It is in the corner,
The farthest uppermost
Of my messy mind,
That perhaps I do not have
Early onset A's.

Maybe my memory jabs,
Word hesitations,
Enunciation miscues,
Forgetfulness—the lot
Is extended brain fog.
The residue of anesthesia intake

During aortic-valve exchange—
An overload on a compromised porous brain.
Or maybe it's my system suffering from not enough
Nutrients—the green and gluten thing.
Ahhh—perhaps—**it is merely old age!**

Would that change what's happening to me?
Is it better to have dementia than
The starting of A's?
No, but it would be wonderfully awesome
To gracefully accept old age—and I promise I will—
I've always felt extremely lucky,
Showing no bad joints or wrinkles
But what does it matter—one for the other?

Oh-e-e-e—just think,
Whaaat if ... several months ago,
I had taken the drugs
From the crisp white-coated neurologist

Pen perched, ever so ready to prescribe?

What happens to those of us—
Taking wrong drugs for something
We don't even have?!
Are we helped in any ol' way?

Am I in total denial right now?
Am I?

I change moods with the wind,
But would you understand if I shared,
In this moment on this day,
It's only my fear of A's inspiring
These anguished tears to drop.
I'm scared.

Nancy Nelson was living in a small bedroom community outside Seattle when her family enticed her to migrate to Las Vegas nearly fifty years ago. Recently retired from a well-known insurance company and ready to relinquish her fast and furious pace, Nancy claims a calmer, quieter life as a writer. She has taken several writing classes, worked with a writing coach, and attended the Wordcrafters Writing Conference in Eugene, Oregon. This is her first book of poetry.

She can be reached at **nancy@BlueRiverApple.com.**

CPSIA information can be obtained
at www.ICGtesting.com
Printed in the USA
FSOW03n0900190515
7268FS